Virology

Mary Buchinger

LILY POETRY REVIEW BOOKS

Contents

CYNOSURE

deer –   sleek supple light
          in the woods – hesitates

          then leaps   taking the eye
     into an ecology of movement

     a breathing heartbeat liquid
       form pouring elegant
     between trees

          ¤

     the eye
a kind of bullet

wherever it
enters makes
     a center

          an apparent horizon
     where light separates

               wick
     in the middle of the candle

          ¤

I am a body of those
who love me
               they live inside

the deer in the woods of me
brings me curious into contact
and materialization   the gift of that

to read and be read   shot through
with a knowing   the world goes in
mysterious   make of it what you will

          ◻

My mother said to use a spade
to divide my clump of bleeding hearts

I choose my narrowest shovel and bury its blade
   in the center of the clutch of roots

    the cupped scoop cuts across   not down
     clips their length

                  in my crude spring
   transplantation of hearts from the front
to the backyard I learn

the difference between a shovel and a spade:
   the angle of the fall from the handle

          ◻

   (at the center
   of each galaxy
   is a black hole
the man on the radio said)

◻

For a while the mystery of the dead
robin under our yew becomes
a center its radius extending
to the yard next-door

with each storm the robin's body
melts into the soil new ivies quilt
across the rusty chest and ebony beak

another robin sometimes comes stands
at the perimeter   tilts its head listening

◻

Horizon separates
the trajectories
of light

deer:
stillness-to-flash
flash-stilled

◻

Each center within
a radius of meaning

(methane hotspots
nuclear test sites

wind shifts the radius of cancer
money shifts
the fallout)

The pandemic too is a picture –

a Venn dance of pink radii
across the map of the world

Centers proliferate

a third eye is *necessary*

an *epicenter*
situated above
the true center
of disturbance

◻

At the center of the car the driver.
no. the passenger.   no. the cash
that passes hand to hand.
no. the distance traveled.
no. the road
between the wheels.

◻

At the center of the sun
is a hole in the retina

light stings its receptor
fire licks the wick

the soul, it burns inside

◻

(What will you teach us, O Pandemic?

What centers will vie? What revolution

will win?   Around what will it spin?)

◻

Rain concentrates a feeling
(radiating ache
marrow traces
the glassy bone)

the body a corporal administrator
of production and goods

head and heart threaded
throughout   venal   arterial

◻

The blossoms on my peach tree wait
for the bees each ruffled shirt unbuttoned

rain and snow and sleet have saturated
the pink blush bees in abeyance

How specific some needs are   coming
with their calling cards their tiny windows
of availability they have a certain radius
the sun knows   the wound-up earth gets it

   Like a toddler the blossoms insist
   Pollinate me now or I will bear no fruit!

        ◻

  All over the state the old
biology is learning the new weather
and the radius of possibility grows
lopsided

     the universe it seems
has an up and a down an undreamed of
directionality we thought it was just
more and more expanding out
from an event

      this the afterglow of the party
aura and aurora   spilled Milky Way
  lighting up this livable place

      our Little Gidding
     the end of all our exploring

◻

Five days of 60° my mother said *Then
you'll find morels* (and if those days
happen in March instead of May?)

      the mushrooms know
they feel the soil the earth tells them
when to grow

◻

What to make of the voice its radiating
     nature   timbre and frequencies
the swallowing of the upper and the lower

the lessening that's inevitable   the pruning
  of the infant mind the narrowing of possibility

◻

Once I was an astronaut of the brain devising
exercises and traps reflective mirrors to light up
    deep cerebral corners   the mystery
     of the corpus collosum – that center of
    the split brain its tuning fork structure
its allowance of cognitive frequencies

I studied the loss of category and number
       the geography of capacity
          the shape of the whole

I feasted on
meanings so small
as meaning is   its little bits   hoof and leaves
genome and Virus   seconds and minutes

◻

It turns out galaxies are larded with black holes
like respiratory droplets in air   they are everywhere
we're just beginning to see –

and one is visible even to the naked eye
via a path in neighboring stars
(on the artist's rendering, the black hole is painted red)

A black hole doesn't swallow every star in its vicinity
which is why we didn't know it was there
said the astronomer   it doesn't
behave as we thought so we missed it

its density isn't absolute
all along it has been there breathing darkness
in the swaying forest of stars

◻

EDGE

A suspension of hens'
minced kidneys laid bare
the intricacies of Virus

   organism at the edge of life
 haunts infects insinuates
(as soul surrounds body)

with a memory in its palm
 it replicates like nesting dolls a swirl
  of oil and pigment in water don't ask
   what's real

   ¬

 My sleeping mind searches
to place the sound of feet –
 going up the stairs or down?

listens as the sound comes closer
 then I test the unknown
  calling out my child's name

   No answer

My love and I in the treachery of dreams
our limbs frozen defenseless
 It opens the door
  enters our bedroom

     a lithe being
barely distinguishable from the night

                                    it leans
over my love as if to take him away
then I know it is Death

    I cry out   grasp my love's hand
he murmurs from his pillow
    and Death leaves

            ¬

    The dream is a scientist
revealing the infection
 that lurks within

    opportunistic organisms
bloom in my house of feeling

            ¬

Some things can't live
outside something living

What separates Virus
                        from emotion from
                        dream from memory
    is a lively field
of associations

        and its wake

    each finally known by its effects

A narrow Fellow in the Grass…
His notice instant is –

¬

     Oh the agility and extravagance
of Virus!

   multiplying via entanglement

           like love
        anger   evocation

Virus recruits life
in its remaking

   like a dream
   assembled in
   the factory
   of sleep –

each night a life from within

   and at its very edge –

¬

The non-negotiable truths? Oh *Beauty*
says Elizabeth Bishop *one of the eternal absolutes*

The very suggestion of beauty being in
the eye of a beholder drove her weeping
to a glass of gin she could not bear it

 And I wonder can I?

                ⌐

The self at attention
feels its interdependence
and attunes to another frequency
1 315 8 11 995 2395

                ⌐

I will take the leftover chicken from the bone
 two grilled drumsticks and mix it with rigatoni
 celery   fresh mint and oregano from the garden
 curry and mayo   This is my proposal
My love says *No the chicken is too good for that*

                ⌐

At the edge of life
    where life is earth
 what are humans?

If the house is life
 what are its people?

what junctures and
intercourse? what odd
and singular beings
intersect and make
meaning?

such dependencies

         ⌐

We need work gloves from Home Depot
and paint some grout A list would be good
so we're prepared and not wandering about
(our masks still made of cloth)

         ⌐

What a million plants look like
was last night's project

This   no *This* The plot size
growing   A million a million
imagine a *Million!*

My mind has to go into hyperdrive
enter a different space and mode
to consider beyond what it can see
and hold   it has to get religious
to imagine a *million*

         ⌐

At the edge of life what is poised there
 at the lip

the sun too must be taken in   the ash tree
lifts new leaves cups of light (borer at bay)

¬

A spiderweb twenty feet away
bounces light off its edge
weaves branch to limb

What will it catch
        what living nutritious thing?

 Make an edge
  and invite in

¬

All the points of contact:

the cat on my thighs
 her ribs against my ribs
  paws hooked over my forearm
   her head against my chest
    she makes a pocket of my seated body;
     the two of us in the wicker loveseat
    on the three-season porch
   in the pocket of morning sun
  spring birds in the blue spruce
 the new leaves of the ash
pocket the light

Virus has to go *inside* life
to do anything at all.

Julian of Norwich says
    there is no inside
    or outside of God

God is in everything
Everything is in God
God transcends
and encloses
all that is made

God doesn't stand
at the edge of life
God is life
Is love

The two doves in the ash
peck at each other
      peck about the head and neck
    jerky urgency   one mounts
    the other   they separate
quick grooming glancing
        touch   rapid
    tip of beak to the other
  then they move apart
spread tailfeathers
peck at themselves preen
  one turns its back

now both turn away
peck at their bodies as if to remove
what just happened
      distance between them
more   then   more
      then one flies out of sight
followed long seconds after by the other

              ⌐

(maybe this is what divine means:

              no edge

today I read Trees may live forever)

              ⌐

The leaf discovered by light
revealed by light invents light

how it filters sun sun-pressed veins
spreading leaf glorified   transfigured
on the limb   a wedge of light

translucent
(the skin of my grandmother's hands)

              ⌐

A hurricane
edge and eye
worlds apart

occupy different economies

the affordances of calm the turbulence
surrounds

Edge is not in
is migrant
is want
peckish

        ¬

Last night H. showed me
her cover letter for a submission
of her work:

"Dear Editors,

        I am liberating these poems
        for your consideration. School."

When I wake I think *Yes. She will school them.*

(Her poems are my school.
I love her school.
I want to go there every day.)

        ¬

Flame lifts
    off the fireplace log
riffs catching its own
drift arias reach
    away semi-trans-
parent blue orange
yellow red embers
  burnt-black log grey
      ash   this edge
bridged breached
     oxidizing

a chemical reaction
combining of elements

Fire at the edge of tree?
No oxygen at the edge
  of stored-away life

What gets it to catch? To leap
     from this to that?
  (I must look this up)

           ¬

My hip on the old futon reminds me
I am not asleep body and mind
fly together no one flies solo
in this encumbered life the shadow
of the window is the window
its moon-bright rectangles stay on the wall
the mind travels along through hot cold hot
foot outside the blanket then in

on my back on my side hip says *I am*
a bone the futon does not love my body of edges
mind at the cusp of sleep actively words
so many things sensemaking it can't help
but thrill to confident all this brilliance
like the moon will follow it into morning –

    the dream catches

           flames

      flames out

     ¬

What is it? the woods ask
Why don't you see us?

We are as intricate and
tangled as your brain

We are green and green
gold and silver light
and green

We say it is time
The time of growth
is every day

    ¬

The dog says *Something will come*
Something good is bound to appear
at the end of your hand   I will rest
full of anticipation   I will close my eyes
and rest waiting

⌐

The fire finds the fat
       heart of the log
     and lingers
           glowing
   amid the ash
of the already-burnt

⌐

I was going to go swimming
     and got waylaid

   Are there really leopards here?

    I venture alone into the twilit village
   quiet in blue dusk lavender sky
a leopard appears sleek low to the ground
  tail flicks seductive stalking

    I am the prey! I yell grab a rock
  chase it up a leafless tree
its yellow-orange body flames
    on a writhing black branch

I run back to safety
So scary I tell the others
we sit shoulder to shoulder
on a wooden bench

I describe what I saw in the half-night
Someone puts a dog on my lap
a small ember to comfort me

    ⌐

The ocean that haunts me
appears tonight on my left
I weigh the possibility of going in
admire its strength and beauty
its wild waves break themselves
against porous volcanic rocks

I study the sand the shallows the shifting
tide   imagine the water against my skin
the buffeting of my insular body

I stand at the edge   waiting

    ⌐

NOVEL

listening I pause
beneath an impotent plum tree

its purple rags fray above my head
the day is almost done

the sky lets go of
the last of its light

a bird repeats
its farewell over
and over as if
not ready yet
to give it up

a man on the abandoned tennis courts
explains what happened to *the shares*
It is what it is

a woman walks the middle
of the darkening street
tells her phone *Yes I understand*

/

I've told you this before my love says *at first*
they did everything with the same equipment –
downhill cross-country jumping –

then just before WWII they put in lifts
and there was a bifurcation

They started making skis that could
go faster on the flats and
specialized boots for downhill

Now each sport has its own equipment

/

Generation: Latin *generăre*
   meaning "to beget"

whole chapters of Genesis
    trees and trees
      of *begats*

          to be in order
          in order to be

/

it's in the middle of the sidewalk.
a small grey box on legs. an oval hole
in one vertical face. its edges carved smooth.
a large yellow sponge inside.

the finish strange. a kind of thickness.
uniform grey. a rough paintable skin.
I want to touch it.

the legs are cocky. such an angle!
sharp departure from the box.

where could I put it? upstairs or downstairs?
would it fit beside the bed? I like it.

What do you think of that? A man asks me.
I hadn't seen him. He's leaning against a truck.
I made that out of a chair. I keep my tools in the box.
Did you see that hole? That is the exact shape
of the tube for cement. I set the bag on top.

I say You knew what you needed and built it.
Yes he says *I think the architect Walter…*
what was his name? Walter Gropius. I think
he would have approved. Yes   I agree   it has
a bit of the Bauhaus to it. *Exactly* he says.

I say I love it when something is so specifically
made to suit a purpose.

Thanks for asking about it he says.
Thanks for telling me I reply.

/

[a video of some sort with a red arrow to click.
the title at the bottom: *Steve Explains God.*
12 minutes.

I'm intrigued.
wonder if my husband made it.
I'll watch it later.]

/

Almost daily I wandered
in Boomerangs and Goodwill
searching rummaging through
poised for the rush of finding
something novel stylish
slightly outrageous
to wear in the world

Is that new? my friend will ask.
I want to say *I'm new.*
Each time.

/

the new therefore always appears in the guise of a miracle

/

What do you get for a five-year-old? I asked my mother.
This was before I had my own children.

Anything she said. *Everything is new to the child.*

/

The new is the shock
that burns in a memory.

The feeling of first.

The tyranny of new.

/

Give it to the baby! the Nigerian women
at the park picnic table instruct the older
children   whatever they are fighting over
Give it to the baby!

/

the very first cell qua cell
depended on the invention
of its membrane;

self-containment gave rise
(some say) to the original life
in the broil of the deep-sea vents

/

For *novel* to get to pandemic
it's a matter of trial and error.
luck and pluck. tested persistence.

if I were asked
this is what I'd offer as proof
Virus is alive

/

the morning self edges into the world.

I must reckon with
what's invisible. the most
of it beyond me. faith being
I can't know what I don't.

/

the spiderling

lifts a leg to test the wind
 spins a span of silk

 then releases its hold
  on what is solid

   pulled along
    a mile high in the sky

        the spiderling
       crosses the ocean

/

Viktor Frankl said, Imagine
asking a world chess master
what is the *best* chess move.

/

What
   if not contingent?

This life I'm born to.
asks me each moment.
asks me. this life asks.
the question never
changes. and so I must.

/

The host cells are changed
  by Virus   microscopically
        visible changes

horizontal transfer
of genetic material
    promotes
the maintenance
of a universal life
biochemistry

kiss kiss deeper and more

/

a blue green yellow-edged
bruise on the plane of my thigh
imparted by the corner of the kitchen table
  visible record of energy transfer   kinetic
accident of bodies in space felt impact
  movement caught and stamped the living
blood (trapped damage) the color of change
vivid as an autumn leaf then fading
back to what was before   a season
of skin documenting what happened

  pond's surface re-coalescing after the disturbance
of a tossed stone   rings hastening into rings
    lap of the shore wet onto dry

      passes unremembered

            /

The instructor said
  think about someone you love

  fill yourself with their love
  picture how you are loving together
  the loving ways you have with each other

    breathe in their love for you
    breathe out your love for them

  Now seated in love seeded with love
  imagine your adversary
    can you direct your love
      to that person?

(and if today
my adversary
is also the one
I love?)

/

*Why can't you just accept
some things are what they are
and will not change?* asks my love

/

*truth lies in the search
for the object*

    not in the object

/

the fluff of a dandelion
  (its pappus filaments)
cups to form a vortex
    whirling it miles away
       from its origin

  such a perfect shape
of emptiness
  within its strands

/

Well, he started feeling bad last fall
more tired than usual, had some pain
thought it must be a hernia
   went to the doctor in December
and that was when they said
it was pancreatic cancer
   he took one treatment
and they did an MRI
   then they said it was
         Everywhere

/

Grace is

   the permanent
   new:

      eternally young
      new every day—
      for every day

/

To each moment I bring
all of what has taken place

the moment asking
something new of me

how can I know
unless I listen?

The shape of my ear
decides what it will hear

  allowance of the possible

            /

        Night said
        You are a flower

    and my genus Rosa name
was revealed to me

(briefer than I'd imagined)

            /

CORONA

        radiant blurry
halo they saw limning
the virion's dark center
        as light escapes
  an eclipsed sun

the researchers a woman
and a man named it *corona* –
crown   garland   wreath

                *

Halo *hello!*
   aura of glory
   divine luster
   crown of light

   signature
   of the Sacred

                *

Benvenuto Cellini the sculptor
the murderer believed his halo
most visible immediately
before sunrise and sunset
and in the drier climate of France

I know what he meant
I've felt it in the holiest
of moments when
I too am holy

Look for it, friends
I want to say
Look for the Light
that surrounds me

*

Last night   my love and I were
lying together in the back of a hearse

sky trees sunshine flashed
through the long low windows

Dry run, he joked
I laughed and reached for his hand

We are foolish, I think
foolish, foolish people after all.

*

She wore the university seal
like a halo an electronic backdrop
Zoom background

   her head protruding into
   the company logo
   I am one of them

*

Crowning is the natural way
a mammal enters the world

    a ring of fire

something material
cedes burning
as it makes room

    *

Virus rattles its crown
and replicates

Where shall I put all the crowns?
the body wants to know

The organs fed up shut down

    *

Magnified

  it's petaled or spiked
a medieval weapon

(nimble clever brute)

  iron morning-star
poised to flail

or a hot cinnamon
candy each carnelian
club   a burst of flavor

I imagine working it
with the tongue

the rough   pleasing
mouth-feel

*

Sticky burr ball
Let's play catch!

an indoor game
with Velcro cells

each of us so well
-equipped

*

Family tree:

Coronaviruses constitute
the subfamily *Orthocoronavirinae*
in the family *Coronaviridae*
in the order *Nidovirales*
and realm *Riboviria*

each known
by relation
to other

      *

*Within the past 24 hours, our Institution has been made aware
of social media activity around our community that violates our
core values of respect, diversity, and inclusion, and our policies
on discrimination.*

*Individuals who further the oppression of those from histori-
cally marginalized groups will not be allowed a place in our
community.*

      *

The putrid smell of the mangled body
overwhelmed me last night

the vicious murder shook me
and I waked to the stink

      *

Reign rain
each drop a crown
on the pool of water

Crater of displacement
within a rise of spires

*

Creeping Jenny –
the green weave
of this weed
below the blooming periwinkle
depends on its scouts
to pop up their periscopes
and grow broadleaved platters
   crowns of chlorophyll
      keep the whole
         body going

   *

The squirrel on the roof next door
yells at me stands up like a squire
looking down at me on the deck
its deck attached to the house *its house*
I'm in its way   whatever I am
I should *go away.*

   *

Supremacy is a convenient thing
an ungodly business
where God is unnatural

   *

When I grow up
I want to be a car
  my son told me

    (and I a non-driver
    was his declaration an indictment
    a hitch a clue?)

What does it feel like to be plastic?
he asked one day   kneeling on the seat
of the subway train

            he stroked the Naugahyde
as the walls of the tunnel
blinked by

        I don't know I said
not sure I could even imagine
inhabiting the promised eternity
    the life after life after life
of those colorful cold molecules

      *

Symbiosis is the other way –

  a fairer house of beehive walls
humming bodies warm in winter
summers of cool winged-motion
a honeyed house with a green green roof –

  this is where I want to live

*

Why are there countries? my son asks

*

The width of a dandelion leaf
depends on the amount of sunlight
it receives at a certain stage
of its development   a critical period
during which the shape of its mature leaf
is determined

*

On a trail in Concord
a beech grows out
from the crook of an oak

they extend up as if one tree
with two dissimilar trunks

in the notch of their separation
someone's placed a painted rock:

Love it says in blood-red.

*

Derek Chauvin killed George Floyd
by kneeling on his neck for 8 min 46 sec

(five hundred twenty-six mississippis
fifty-two rounds of happy birthday
twenty-six hand-washings)

*Chauvinism is an irrational belief
in the superiority or dominance
of one's own group or people*

        *

When I lived in the Andes I was tall
and white I was no longer me

I was wanted at the tables of rich people
Touch her the children were urged

I was the object of my skin
I was a blue carnation

        *

the eye is not
the I of inside

when the eyes
change do I?

        *

Whose birth
  in the crowning?

Whose crown?

Who's crowned?

                    *

Virus is equipped for movement
and dominance   a well-armed
protein (have you been crowned?
the crown can take you down)

                    *

            In the gospel of revolution
            the crown is made of thorns

            a baby is the powerful one
                the Magi bow to

                    *

It was a false spring
someone kept rising
only to be told *Too soon*!

Too soon!
What does truth
know of time?

      *

as I prayed
my body
became moss-
green light
of the earth
above the earth

      *

the gibbous June moon
cut through the thunderhead

jailbreak moon searchlight moon
in its wake light-crowned shards of cloud

      *

My grandfather planted his fields
with an eye on the moon

  counted the stars within its halo
to reckon the coming days of rain

      *

Yesterday I stood in the median
of Massachusetts Avenue
holding a sign of protest

my body a weapon   physical presence
its stamp on space   self-evident truth

I felt flimsy as my sign
as slight as vulnerable
a dandelion beside the ditch
bowing in the breeze of cars

another summer afternoon
when I was a child I rode
beside my father on a tractor
mowing down fragrant
gold-headed weeds

the old sadness rising

Justice => Peace

pipe dream   pie in the sky   hope against hope   castle in the air
     (why so many expressions for this?)

a sun a son uneclipsed

                    *

VIRUS

In this world of scientific possibility,
Virus has three Origin Stories:

1. a shadow of its former self

2. escaped / went rogue

3. here first / ever since / all along

-

Sugar-coated
Virus comes knocking

sweetness its key
for entry

once inside the cell
replication begins

-

Virus
    (organism
at the edge
    of the living)

asks

what qualifies
as *alive?*

—

One test of life
is the clouding
of a mirror
    breath visible
     evidence

       yet unless there's a witness

(someone to watch and press *Record*

  to hold and read the mirror –

the mirror itself indifferent)

what can be known
with certainty?

—

And this is why the need
to stay awake

     Gilgamesh
had only to keep
   from sleep
    for seven nights

      and Eternal Life
    would have been his!

(which he got   tho not the kind he'd imagined;
his doomed quest so human so *relatable*
it lives & lives!)

      -

Being kept awake
is a form of torture

Does Virus sleep?
A sign of life

       I keep looking

       It keeps looking

      -

(Finger poised to press RECORD)

(

human knee on human neck

someone must listen
as a dying man criesout
to his dead mother;

                  -

)

      -

What is that which *separates*
Virus from the life
it inhabits?
                  what is that
which *joins*?

                  -

    The cabbie in Kalamazoo said
there could be no posh St. Joseph
without broke Benton Harbor

Twin cities don't both grow

            the rich fill their pockets
            with the poor

            -

There are recipes
for everything

            the deer tick for example
            is so well put together

    its sharp-toothed probes
anaesthetize then saw
      into the skin
embed deeper and deeper
to get the sturdy hold it needs
    to exchange saliva
    for blood

              (water for
    oil / water for wine)

when the blood
    hits the tick's system
it activates
    the Lyme bacterium

        a witches' brew
    that can take a day or two –
how necessary that sturdy hold

        -

What is touched that blooms in response?

        -

The Bricks is hard. It's hard…I mean, look at where we standing at, right? – you know, where poverty is real.

The George that I met was a man who had all the stripes, who had all the scars and scratches and the war wounds and who could speak from a place of experience and say… I've walked down this path…This isn't the way.

So the George Floyd that I met was an advocate for change.

        -

The ant strokes the aphid
extracts a sweetness
  it can live on

ferries the aphid
  from shriveled leaf
  to fresh crisp new

                  -

(the extra whipped cream
        the leftover I'd planned on
        with strawberries –
  my love ate it   it's gone)

                  -

My friend made a bird sanctuary
in her tiny backyard   a cake of suet
a glass jar of sugar water with spouts for hummingbirds
and a bath

she watched as
  a cardinal pecked at the cake
  and sang in the tree

  a squirrel clung to the cage
    upside-down   nipped at the suet
      making her laugh!

then she spotted
a small rat   *kind of cute*
sneak beneath the leaves
of the false Solomon's seal

(*Don't tell B*, she warns)

-

What's a body, but a habitat?

   7% of the human genome is made of
      ancient viruses

                  the soul too
a home
         what legions lodge inside –
            exorcise   exercise

-

(the second life vest we ordered
came in the mail while we were away

sat in a box on our porch
                  and nobody stole it)

-

We've never seen three deer along the highway
on this trip before, my love says

                              I've never really looked
so closely, I tell him.

    Maybe they're always here and only sometimes we see

how much we miss   not looking

                -

Virus does what it's ~~made~~ ~~designed~~
learned to do   its marching orders:
    replicate and replicate till thwarted

Like a corporation Virus is not alive
    and can't be killed only cast out
        like devils into a sounder of swine

        Virus must live somewhere
        It requires a host

                -

from the Latin neuter vīrus *referring to poison*
and other noxious liquids, from the same
Indo-European base as Sanskrit viṣa, *Avestan*
vīša, *and ancient Greek* ἰός *(all meaning poison)*

                -

Just because you can't see it
  doesn't mean it's not there

The ones who don't know
                they have it
  are shedders and spreaders too

ignorance ≠ innocence

        -

My dream makes clear
there is but one moment
and one place

            the missing of this
        nexus
        proves fatal to the mission

        No second chances

        -

The skin is the largest organ

    nostrils and mouth
      are entry points
  to lungs to gut to inside

Virus has learned
   Success = Succession

-

I crouch on the stony bank
  of Little East Pond

and watch something
   pick its way on insect legs
across the drying body of a slug

What I see is a trembling triangle
   more motley more grey
      than dirt than bark

   and suddenly it opens
  into twin rooms of blue

  winged sapphire surprise
   spilled and contained

  opening-closing-opening
it flutters away out of my sight

-

Adorno writes *the abolition of fear
is the task of the revolution*

-

Marguerite Duras tells
how she interrogated an informer
  during the Occupation:

    he is naked and pitiful
      I am a white brow
    my eyes hidden in the shadow
    cast by a hurricane lantern
    trained on his shriveled testicles

What color is your identity card? I ask
  he does not answer

    at my direction two men
  methodically beat and kick him

blow by blow he gets separated
  from the rest of humankind

some women watching
  can take no more
    and leave

      (O Adorno
      For *whom* will there be
      no fear?)

  The person who tortures the informer is me.

  So also is the one who feels like making
  love to Ter, the member of the Militia.

I give you the torturer
         along with the rest of the texts.

Learn to read them properly:
    they are sacred

-

Only this is what it means to be
human what gets asked everyday
every moment of every day
what gets asked is what it means
what is human what am I
what's at the edge is it alive?
Mirror Mirror?

-

All of it each piece the suet the lung the republic
        the holy communion of humanity
                        asks its everyday question

-

A break in the integrity of the skin
    and infection comes creeping in

-

In my dream I had COVID
I was traveling
   had to get back
      on a plane with others
            I was unraveling
sickness   still in the early stages wondering
what's to come
       what to do with my body
   my dangerous body

-

(what can't be seen
  only experienced)

-

breath betrays

    droplets
spewed out breathed in
word highway exit entry

The word stands in for the object.
So the words you choose must be perfect.

The world is charged with language

-

My neighbor Rachel has a two-year-old and a newborn
    her in-laws from China are quarantined with them
in the condo   her husband takes walks with their son
    they stop under my spruce each morning to talk
to the broken *fawn* with painted plaster chunking off
its bare iron stem leg   and two ceramic *frogs* who
sit on their haunches as if ready to spring from the block
of slate dark as a pond beside a blue glass *whale* and
a *clay pot* with a *rainbow* of child-markings and an earthen
rabbit wrapped in periwinkle   they come by every day
stand beside the menagerie and discuss their impressions
    the language of father teaching the world and son learning
I don't understand the words   still I know what they're saying
the patient repetition call and response and I think What shall I
add for tomorrow? What new word for this child to learn?

-

Empathy, I say   and my student says, Yes, but how much
and how long?

        How can I feel every time and keep feeling?

Every moment, a new image of suffering. So many feels.
            I just can't any more.

-

Be rooted like a tree in the midst of life
the instructor tells me

Stand in the field of noise
Hear how the noise is a fulness of silence

-

In my sleep   strangers
come to search for ticks

patient they examine my skin

they find one on my forehead
near the part in my hair

they rub and rub   try to dislodge it

It's embedded I say

Together we work to extract it

-

PANDECT

It enters through the eyes
  the ears   the skin

You give it by speaking
You get it by listening

It is communicable
 a hazard of being

            x

The way to trace it

   (as in draw lines
   connecting here
   to there)

is called 'history'

it's objective
and abstract

(unless you're its subject)

            x

The smallest act in the most limited circumstances
bears the seed of the same boundlessness,

because one deed, and sometimes one word,
suffices to change every constellation.

x

A purple Columbine strayed
        beyond its garden
    into a crack in the city
        sidewalk

I wanted it
  touched it
  almost tested its roots

if I took this Beauty home
  it would be mine alone

x

I diagram sentences
they turn into labyrinths
  within labyrinths

I can see from above
  yet am lost inside

a rat shall lead me
shall follow its nose

    its predilection for left or right
    stems from the union
    of the sperm and egg
    from which it descended

(a jealous God, visiting
the iniquity of the fathers
upon the children)

genetic inheritance
unfolds

     (revelation upon
revelation)

         within a landscape

         (its loops and traps)

          pre-sculpted

     x

         whatever you say
it was there before it's part of
         something larger

     x

My love he blames everything
on the Genesis *begats*

If you can stand to read all the begats
then you can think any damn thing

No, not just any
but that people will get sick
there is nothing we can do

People will get shot
there is nothing we can do

(this-and-this-and-this
no because no why no if–)

                    x

(At some point Elizabeth Bishop
decided she no longer had to "regard
every poem as something almost absolutely new...
[it's] all really one long poem anyway")

                    x

From the end of my block
  an ugly sound of dogs snarling
then charging violent engagement

I can't see only hear the growling
and chomping of teeth A woman comes
running calling frantic frightened
Whitey! Stop it Whitey! Whitey! Come here!

My neighbor Willie struggles with his two
manic leashed dogs who can barely stand
each other let alone some free strange other

I imagine him pulling them hard
trying to disengage their frenzy
as he yells at the woman

> *Are you some kind of special?*
> *Put your dog on a leash*
> *or get off my street!*

x

Whatever the bullet
  it must be magic
    to not be tragic

  to impart without
parting   to insinuate
itself with good violence
  as in the best of fables

  to destroy only what is
destructive and to spare
  the spark

x

An adolescent raccoon banished
from its family found our comfy couch
beneath a rain-cover on the deck

It crawled inside and later emerged
to be found out by our two cats
behind a glass door who discovered
within themselves otherworld voices
guttural uttering   incantatory warning

The raccoon came closer to look
What's that noise?

Four eyes flashed back at it tails flared
    the cats fizzed and popped!

The raccoon stood up blinked
presented its clean open paws
See? No weapon! driving the cats
into further madness and finally
the racoon clambered onto the railing
clumsy sleepy made its way to the ground

Community policing, my love observed
when the cats finally settled down

                    x

You can read the history of sight and sound
in plants and every creature and stone

                    x

Perched on a rock beside
a clear mountain pond
  I watch a tiny shadow
    creep from out of shadow

a comic-strip silhouette
its triangle head swivels
as if tuning in to its surround

its four feet touch lightly
              on ribboned sand
release tiny silt clouds flecks of mica

    then its legs lift like wings and tuck in
against its supple undulating center

  a long muscular tail (where exactly
does it begin?) propels this liquid being
    through liquid
                  legs not helpless
          direct the flow over its body
          maneuvering deftly from here
to there feet down it gazes around

  curious   hunting
          from within the cleft of a rock

subtle movement   it's swimming again
                  and I want to know

What are you? creature   moving
    below the surface with every
        possible advantage   comical   wary
      graceful   between sun and shadow

        x

  two sisters in red t-shirts
fly through the street
on silent bikes

their silver spokes
flick the sun

the trees and I wave
as they weave their way

x

One August morning I look up
into the juncture between sky and roof

and see fluff-ferried seeds –
filaments burnished with sun – shivers of light

they don't know they are shining
don't know they are broken

I call to my love   *Come look!*
                    Sit here beside me and Look!

floss and flecks   spider silk   motes
shuttle above our heads in the ocean of air

It must always be like this   we say –

sun-silvered streams trajectories expanding –

every moment of every day   and only
sometimes the light   our relation to the light
               is just right so we can see *really see!*

x

My friend and I walk together
    beside our favorite fenny pool
      at the city edge

Tall pale torches of flowers flame
    in new summer grass

    ecclesiastical buzz and flurry
damselflies phoebes wrens

My friend too inhabits the fullness
Everything she says *has its time.*

      x

I dream I have the power to make her young again

  the daughter I never had or is it a nation? playing hide-and-seek
mine to find   among the trees

and I lift this small being laughing high above my head
Such strength and joy!

I hold the myth against the sky   in my arms
  a weighted measure of something impossible

asleep in the dream of me it breathes

      x

Notes

"Cynosure"

The possibility of directionality in the universe was reported by researchers at the University of New South Wales in April, 2020.

The reference to "Little Gidding" and quote are from T. S. Eliot, *The Four Quartets*.

In the spring of 2020, researchers detected a black hole within 1,000 light years of earth; https://www.eso.org/public/archives/releases/sciencepapers/eso2007/eso2007a.pdf.

"Edge"

The definition of a virus as an "organism at the edge of life" comes from a research article by Ed Rybicki in *South African Journal of Science*, 1990.

Section four contains a quote from Emily Dickinson's poem, "A narrow Fellow in the Grass" (1096).

The anecdote about Elizabeth Bishop being upset during a discussion of beauty is from the biography by Megan Marshall, *Elizabeth Bishop: A Miracle for Breakfast*, 2017.

Julian of Norwich was a religious mystic who lived in England in the Middle Ages.

"Novel"

Viktor E. Frankl in his book, *Man's Search for Meaning*, discusses the impossibility of talking about the "meaning of life in general;" he suggests we can only talk about "the specific meaning of a person's life at a given moment." He elaborates: "Ultimately, man should not ask what the meaning of his life is, but rather he must recognize that it is he who is asked. In a word, each man is questioned by life; and he can only answer to life by answering for his own life; to life he can only respond by being responsible."

The quote regarding horizontal gene transfer (HGT) is from the Wikipedia entry on HGT.

Hannah Arendt wrote, "The new always happens against the overwhelming odds of statistical laws and their probability, which for all practical, everyday purposes amounts to certainty; the new therefore always appears in the guise of a miracle."

The identification of truth with the search for it was made by Søren Kierkegaard and discussed in the book, *Idea-Men of Today,* by Vincent Edward Smith, 1950, p. 254-255.

The quote regarding 'grace' is from Kierkegaard, *Christian Discourses,* April 26, 1848, Lowrie, 1961. Oxford University Press, p. 275-276.

"Corona"

The name "coronavirus" was coined by June Almeida and David Tyrrell who first observed and studied human coronaviruses.

Benvenuto Cellini (1500-1571) was an Italian goldsmith and sculptor who also murdered several people, including the killer of his brother. His belief that he had a halo was recorded in his memoirs.

The institutional statement regarding community values was issued (in an expanded version) by a university in Boston, Massachusetts, in May, 2020.

In Minneapolis, Minnesota, on May 25, 2020, a white police officer, Derek Chauvin, killed a Black man named George Floyd by kneeling on his neck for 8 minutes and 46 seconds.

The definition of Chauvinism was found in Wikipedia.

"Virus"

Most of the facts about viruses and ticks referenced in the poem are from Wikipedia, including the three theories regarding the origin of viruses.

The quote, "The abolition of fear is the task of the revolution," is from Theodor W. Adorno.

Marguerite Duras' description of torturing an informant and of her desire to make love to a member of the Militia is found in *The War* (Barbara Bray, translator; 1985).

The quotes regarding George Floyd's neighborhood and life come from a news story on National Public Radio and were spoken by a teacher who knew Floyd and who works in the neighborhood. [https://www.npr.org/2020/06/09/873377463/george-floyd-friends-and-family-remember-his-life-and-legacy]

Susan Howe said, "The word stands in for the object. So the words you choose must be perfect. The world is charged with language," in the interview, "An Open Field: Susan Howe in Conversation." [https://poets.org/text/open-field-susan-howe-conversation]

"Pandect"

Hannah Arendt wrote, "The smallest act in the most limited circumstances bears the seed of the same boundlessness, because one deed, and sometimes one word, suffices to change every constellation," in her book, *The Human Condition* (1958).

The quote "a jealous God, visiting the iniquity of the fathers upon the children" is from Exodus, chapter 20, verse 5; full verse: "Thou shalt not bow down thyself to them, nor serve them: for I the Lord thy God am a jealous God, visiting the iniquity of the fathers upon the children unto the third and fourth generation of them that hate me."

The quote from Elizabeth Bishop regarding her work being one long poem is taken from the biography by Megan Marshall, *Elizabeth Bishop: A Miracle for Breakfast*, 2017.

Acknowledgements

My heartfelt thanks to the editors of the following publications for including my work:

Tandeta Journal: "Cynosure"

Voices Amidst the Virus: Poets Respond to the Pandemic, Lily Poetry Anthology (Eds. Eileen Cleary and Christine Jones): "Corona" Selections from the anthology were featured in the 2021 Michigan State University Filmetry Festival https://filmstudies.cal.msu.edu/filmetry-festival/.

These poems were written in a world under siege; unlike so many others, I was fortunate to be able to sequester myself in my home. I thank my husband, Steve, who continued to do the grocery shopping and kept me and our household going. Thanks also to Provost Caroline Zeind and Dean Delia Anderson, and to the Massachusetts College of Pharmacy and Health Sciences, for the generous grant of a sabbatical— though it wasn't the sabbatical I had dreamed of, it helped make this work possible. The writing and exploration of these themes benefited from the loving care and insights of my friend, Hilary Sallick, who, just blocks away, met with me on Zoom, as well as for walks to Alewife Brook. I am inspired by Hilary's daily participation in the Black Lives Matter standout in Davis Square, and her insistence on living within the questions. Thanks also to Linda Haviland Conte, poetry sister, for gathering us in community, with tea and treats. I am forever grateful to Eileen Cleary for believing in my work and for encouraging me, and for the expertise and patience of Martha McCollough. Through the many ways my life was made strange to me in the COVID-19 pandemic, I learned what grounds me— the love of my husband, sons, mother, brothers, friends; the companionship of my dog and cats; and long walks under trees.

About the author

Author photo: Kathy L. Dalton

Mary Buchinger is the author of /klaʊdz/(Lily Poetry Review Books 2021), *e i n f ü h l u n g/in feeling* (Main Street Rag, 2018), *Aerialist* (Gold Wake, 2015, finalist for the May Swenson Poetry Award, semifinalist for *The Journal* /Wheeler and Perugia Press Prizes), and *Navigating the Reach* (forthcoming, Salmon Poetry). She grew up in rural Michigan, volunteered in Ecuador for the Peace Corps, holds a doctorate in linguistics from Boston University. Mary serves on the board of the New England Poetry Club and teaches at the Massachusetts College of Pharmacy and Health Sciences. She lives in Cambridge with her husband, dog, and cats.

Website: https://www.marybuchinger.com